Original title:
The Lemon's Spark

Copyright © 2025 Creative Arts Management OÜ
All rights reserved.

Author: Penelope Hawthorne
ISBN HARDBACK: 978-1-80586-345-8
ISBN PAPERBACK: 978-1-80586-817-0

Glowing Nectar

In a citrus land, bright and bold,
A zesty tale is waiting to be told.
With a squeeze and a twist, oh what a sight,
A burst of joy that feels just right.

Dancing on coffee, what a strange blend,
A laugh in the morning, a citrusy trend.
Pies take a spin, with giggles and zest,
In this tangy party, we are all guests.

Juggling fruit, oh what a sight,
With a splash of juice, we take flight.
Sticky fingers and smiles all around,
In this zany world, fun knows no bound.

So raise your glass, let's join the cheer,
In this zesty chaos, we have no fear.
A splash of laughter, a dollop of glee,
In our bright citrus world, forever we'll be!

Radiant Burst

When life gives you zests, you dance and sing,
In this bright garden, laughter takes wing.
With each tiny drop, a giggle will flare,
As we pirouette in the tangy air.

With a wink, the fruit shows its zest,
As it splatters around, making a mess.
Sour and sweet, a comical fight,
In this bubbly realm, everything's right.

Picture a lemon, wearing a hat,
Chasing a lime, don't let it fall flat!
With a raucous twist, they tumble and roll,
Creating a riot, that's their main goal.

So gather your friends for a citrus parade,
With giggles and puns, let's never fade.
In this world of zest, we'll laugh till we drop,
In our wacky, wild, fruity hop!

Refreshing Horizons

A twist of zest in summer's light,
Bright yellow orbs in joyous flight.
They bounce and roll, a playful dance,
With every taste, they take a chance.

Sour faces, then laughter swells,
As sweetened joy in a glass compels.
They giggle in cocktails and pies,
Shining bright, like sunny skies.

Golden Sparks

Citrus bursts, a cheeky grin,
With every slice, the fun begins.
They prank the palates, tease the lips,
In fizzy drinks and juicy sips.

Dancing peels, a vibrant show,
Golden balls of cheer aglow.
They spark the wit and tickle delight,
A fruity feast, from morn till night.

Zesty Horizons

In baskets bright, they sit and glare,
With cheeky pouts, they catch the stare.
Slice a wedge, unleash the grin,
Life's a party when they spin.

They roll and tumble, none are safe,
In juicy games, they carve their waif.
Oh, pucker up, the zest is prime,
Each cheerful bite, a taste of rhyme.

Glimmering Citrus Path

Beneath the sun, they shine so grand,
With fruity friends, a joyful band.
They sneak into desserts with flair,
Creating giggles everywhere.

Lemonade rivers in laughter flow,
While cheeky slices steal the show.
Citrusy winks in every twirl,
A twinkling grin to make you whirl.

Bright Temptations

In a sunlit grove, so juicy and bright,
A citrus toss, what a fruity delight!
With a twist and a squeeze, the laughter does flow,
Who knew a fruit could steal the show?

With each little drop, my tongue does a dance,
A zesty tango, oh what a chance!
I grin from ear to ear, it's quite the sight,
This tangy charmer ignites pure delight!

Vibrant Elixir

A splash of sunshine in a glass so clear,
Mixing giggles and sips, oh bring it near!
With a spritz of joy, bubble up my drink,
Life's too short, just let it wink!

Shaking up fun in every bold swirl,
My fizzy concoction makes the taste buds whirl.
Who needs a party when there's zest in the air?
Pour another round, let's debonair!

Sour Serenade

Beneath this tartness, a melody's spun,
Whistling sweet tunes, oh, let's have fun!
A squeeze and a squint, a playful reprise,
With every sour note, laughter will rise!

In every pucker, a symphony sings,
With playful jabs and bright little swings.
The sweeter the laughter, the bolder the cheer,
Let's squeeze out the fun and spread it here!

Zing of Life

A burst of zest in each lively bite,
This playful fruit keeps spirits alight.
In the dance of flavors, joking takes flight,
With every tart giggle, the world's feeling right!

So pour on the laughter, mix in the cheer,
With every refreshing sip, fun draws near.
Zingy and zesty, what a great spree,
In this tangy adventure, just come and see!

A Splash of Bright

In the kitchen, a twist of fate,
A fruit that's yellow, oh so great.
It rolls and bounces with such cheer,
A dancing globe, let's draw it near.

With citrus giggles, it takes a dive,
In lemonade, the taste alive!
A splash of joy in every sip,
A fruity whirl on a sunny trip.

Sun-Drenched Citrus

Sunshine yellow, bursting bright,
A zesty joke, what a delight!
With every slice, a twist of fun,
A citrus pun under the sun.

We squeeze and squirt, what a scene,
A tangy laugh, so fresh and keen.
In pies and drinks, it plays its part,
A cheeky wink, it steals the heart.

Lively Aroma

In the market, quirks abound,
This little fruit's the funniest around.
A whiff of zest, it plays a song,
A fragrant jest that can't go wrong.

Peeling back layers, it giggles wide,
A splash of joy we can't abide.
In jams and tarts, oh what a show,
This lively bloom steals every glow.

Warm Hues

Warm hues glow in the midday light,
A cheeky surprise, what a sight!
With laughter's tone, it bursts on cue,
A sunny jest, all bright and new.

In tangy bites, we find our glee,
Rolling smiles like waves at sea.
So here's to you, dear citrus friend,
Your golden charm will never end.

Citrus Symphony

In a fruit bowl sat a charm,
A yellow orb with zesty arm.
It danced and twirled upon the shelf,
Making jokes about itself.

With every squeeze, a giggle grew,
As friends all laughed, 'What will you do?'
It shrugged and said, 'Just roll with me,
Life's better with a zesty spree!'

Refreshing Dreams in Yellow

In a dream, I chased a fruit of cheer,
Dressed in yellow, oh so dear.
It slipped and slid across my floor,
Yelling, 'Catch me!' - what a bore!

I grabbed it tight, it squirted back,
Said, 'Let's hit that fruity track!'
We rolled and tumbled, pure delight,
Woke up laughing, what a sight!

Sweet and Sour Harmony

In a kitchen bright and cheery,
Lived a wedge, both bright and leery.
'Half sweet, half sour,' it brightly said,
Making faces, turning heads.

It joined a pie, what a big deal,
Joking, 'I'm the zestful meal!'
With every bite, a laugh would burst,
Yummy chaos, quenched our thirst!

Gleaming Citrus Echoes

A citrus ball, all gleaming bright,
Whispered jokes from morning till night.
It told a tale of a fruit parade,
Of wacky friends that it had made.

With limes as clowns and oranges spry,
They juggled seeds with a silly sigh.
In laughter's grip, they danced away,
Citrus fun, come join the play!

Citrus Canvas

A citrus swirl on canvas bright,
A splash of yellow, pure delight.
The artist's brush dances with glee,
As juicy lemons skip with me.

When life hands fruit with zesty cheer,
We paint our laughter, loud and clear.
Squeezed in humor, dripped in fun,
A tart delight, oh what a pun!

The palette glows with shades so bold,
Each lemon tale a story told.
Giggles bubble, zest takes flight,
In every brushstroke, pure sunlight.

With sticky fingers, we all play,
Mash and mix, what a brighter day!
In a world that's zingy, full of cheer,
Our citrus canvas, ever near.

Bright Horizons

In sunny skies, the jokes take flight,
With every twist, there's sheer delight.
The sun is shining, oh what bliss,
A world of citrus, who could miss?

A slice of zest, a wink, a grin,
As we all frolic, let's begin!
Car wheels dance on lemon peels,
In laughter's grasp, the joy reveals.

Around the bend, the skyline beams,
With fruity dreams and silly schemes.
We embrace the summer, bright and bold,
With every sip, a story told.

Let's raise our glasses, laughter flows,
Together in this, joy surely grows.
The horizon's painted, laughter rings,
In every citrus, humor springs.

Joyful Juice

With every squeeze, the giggles pour,
Joyful juice, who could ask for more?
A splash of flavor, so divine,
In every drop, our spirits shine.

We twirl and twist, the dance begins,
Mixing giggles with our grins.
Lemonade stands, a pirate's gold,
Stories shared, never old.

The blender whirs, a silly song,
With fruits so bright, we can't go wrong.
Straws like rockets, zooming high,
A carnival of laughter in the sky.

So raise your cups, let laughter flow,
In juicy joys, we all will glow.
When life gets zesty, we cannot lose,
Just sip the humor, it's joyful juice!

Nature's Light

In fields of green where giggles sprout,
Nature's light and laughter shout.
Golden fruits on branches sway,
In this funny world, we play.

The garden's chorus, buzzing bright,
With every bloom, pure joyful sight.
Lemon trees, they dance and sway,
With cheeky whispers, come what may.

A fruit parade, a silly race,
Nature's humor, it sets the pace.
Chasing shadows, we take flight,
In every bounce, there shines a light.

So grab a friend, come join the fun,
Beneath the sky, we laugh and run.
With nature's smiles, we find delight,
In every moment, there's pure light.

Sunshine's Fragrance

In a garden where the laughter grows,
Bright yellow smiles where the citrus glows.
Fruit on a tree with a giggling sound,
Bouncing through branches, joy knows no bound.

Peeled with a twist, it dances on air,
Zesty little jokes, without a care.
Squeeze out the juice, let the fun begin,
With every drop, we're guaranteed a grin.

Acidic Dreams

In dreams where fizz and tang collide,
Bubbles of laughter take us for a ride.
A sour-faced villain with a twisty grin,
Pops and zings—let the mischief begin!

Woke up with a chuckle, mouth puckered tight,
Sipping on sunshine, what a silly sight!
Chasing the giggles, so juicy, so bright,
Witty little creatures dance in the light.

Citrus Cascade

A waterfall of zest, oh what a treat,
Dancing like raindrops on nimble feet.
Squirrels with hats join the merry parade,
Frolicking flavors in the lemon glade.

Juggling the fruits, the jester appears,
Swapping sour tales with laughter and cheers.
With every splash, a joke is told,
Rolling on the ground, the humor unfolds.

Luminous Refreshment

A glow in the glass, a fizz in the air,
Sip it quick, it's a laugh to share.
Bright as a wink, with a twist of delight,
Refreshing each moment, pure silly light.

Bendir the fruit, and watch it show off,
Sour like wisdom, but never too soft.
With chuckles that bubble and bubbles that tickle,
Life's zesty moments are surely no trickle.

Citrus Melody

In a grove where puns just grow,
Fruity laughter starts to flow.
Zesty smiles on every face,
Juicy jokes, a citrus race.

Squeezing laughs from every slice,
Tangy wit, oh so nice.
Peeling giggles, oh so bright,
In this fruit-filled burst of light.

Oranges join in with a cheer,
Banana slips appear near.
A citrus band, we all will croon,
Under the warmth of a sunny moon.

Every twist brings silly glee,
In this fruit bazaar, come see!
Dancing zest and laughter shake,
Such sweet humor, for goodness' sake!

Exuberant Glow

A burst of yellow in the sun,
This fruit parade is so much fun.
Twists and puns in every bite,
Sour faces turn to light.

Bouncing jokes upon the vine,
Citrus puns, oh what a shine!
Grapefruits bounce and lemons prance,
Each slice leads to a silly dance.

Fizzy laughter fills the air,
With every zest, there's joy to spare.
A pinch of wit, a splash of cheer,
This fruity feast brings all the dear.

Peel away that frown, don't pout,
In this grove, it's fun, no doubt!
Lemons chuckle, limes cavort,
Join the jest in this sweet sport!

Cheery Citrus Bloom

In a field where smiles abound,
Citrus breezes swirly round.
Punny cornels on the vine,
Brightening up with tangy shine.

Lemons giggle, oranges cheer,
Fruitful fun is finally here!
A citrus cart rolls along,
Full of fruit and silly songs.

Every slice a chuckle brings,
Dancing leaves and fluttering wings.
The juiciest jokes on every road,
In this merry citrus abode.

Playful zest, so carefree,
In this garden of glee.
So let the fruitful fun resume,
In this cheery citrus bloom!

Sour Symphony

In the orchard, discord reigns,
Lemons laughing, shaking chains.
A sour note meets a giggle,
In this zesty, fruity wiggle.

Fiddles come with citrus sound,
Bananas dance, spinning round.
Limes in rows, a funny beat,
Each sour note's a tasty treat.

Trumpets blare with citrus zest,
This fruit ensemble is the best!
Every peel a comic tune,
In the light of a fruity moon.

Sour moments turn to cheer,
In this fruit-filled atmosphere.
A symphony of laughter grows,
In our orchard, anything goes!

Souring into Sweetness

In a garden of citrus, a laugh does arise,
A fruit looking grumpy, with pouting disguise.
It waited and waited, for sunshine and cheer,
Then burst out in giggles, no longer severe.

A twist of a peel, a laugh in the bowl,
Sour and then sweet, it's life's funny role.
It danced on the plate, a zesty delight,
Who knew such a fuss could be simply just right?

Round and around with its pals on the tree,
A rumble of laughter as sweet as can be.
The jokes of the orchard, they'd roll with a grin,
For what once felt so sour, made friendship begin.

So here's to the fruit, in all of its zest,
Turning frowns upside down, it's surely the best.
With every fresh squeeze, a giggle we'll share,
For life's just more fun, with a little flair!

A Burst of Light

In the fridge lies a treasure, so bright and so bold,
A prankster of fruit, with adventures untold.
It hops on the counter, spills juice with a cheer,
A comic explosion, it's laughter we hear.

Oh, the tales it could tell, of splashes and slips,
Of mornings gone wild, of citrusy trips.
It zings through our lives, with a wink and a smile,
Reminding us all to be silly awhile.

With every fresh squeeze, it tickles the taste,
Turning dull moments into zesty haste.
A burst of bright yellow, a twist of pure glee,
Who knew such a fruit could be wild and carefree?

So let's toss confetti, with zest on our face,
And dance round the kitchen, this space is our place.
For in every small bite, a party we'll find,
A burst of pure joy, like sunshine combined!

Limoncello Dreams

In a glass overflowing with golden delight,
There's giggling and swaying, oh what a sight!
It tickles the tongue, paints smiles oh so wide,
Bringing friends together, with joy as our guide.

Imaginations swirl with the sweetest of dreams,
As laughter erupts in citrusy streams.
A sip of the sun, with a twist and a turn,
Each chuckle and sip, for which we all yearn.

Bubbling with bubbles, the fizziness plays,
In a dance of good spirits for lazy sunny days.
With flavors that sparkle, and laughter so free,
It turns every moment to pure jubilee.

So here's to the nights, with limoncello toast,
We'll cheer to the fruit that we all love the most.
In dreams filled with citrus and sweet, zesty schemes,
Life's funny and bright, in our limoncello dreams!

Fragrant Sunlit Paths

On paths kissed by sunshine, the laughter doth bloom,
A zesty wind whispers, dispelling all gloom.
With every bright step, a giggle does weave,
The citrusy vibes that we simply believe.

With fragrant adventures, the day does ignite,
As snickers and chuckles dance into the light.
The trees all are grinning, with lemons to share,
And friendships are sewn in the fresh-scented air.

Oh, the joy of the journey through leaves in a swirl,
With each bouncing step, watch the playful twirl.
Sour or sweet, it matters not now,
For laughter's the essence, and we take a bow.

So stroll through the paths, with a twinkle and grin,
With lemons beside us, let the fun times begin.
For in every sweet moment, let's take on the craft,
Of living our lives, with a hug and a laugh!

Sunshine's Embrace

A citrus twist on a sunny day,
Rolling with laughter in our play.
Bright yellow slices giggle and gleam,
Turning our grumbles into a dream.

Peeled and playful, they dance around,
Making the mundane seem profound.
Sour faces turn to smiling grins,
In a fruity world where fun begins.

Citrus Kaleidoscope

Colors swirl in a fruity show,
Zesty giggles start to flow.
Each wedge whispers a silly rhyme,
Sharing joy, one slice at a time.

Sour notes mix with sweet delight,
A carnival in every bite.
With peel confetti and seeds so bright,
In this zany world, we take flight!

Lively Zest

When life gives you fruit, make it funny,
Turn up the charm, don't be a dummy.
With every drop and every squirt,
We'll wear our laughs like citrus shirts.

Running wild in a fruit parade,
Finding joy in a lemon shade.
Squeezed and jolly, we dance around,
Lively zests in abundance found.

Sweet Sunbeams

Golden beams on citrus bright,
Twisting and turning, oh what a sight!
Sugary laughs in every bite,
Tickles our tummies, pure delight.

Lemonade puddles and sunshine dreams,
Hopscotch giggles and fruit-filled beams.
Waves of laughter in the air,
Sweet and tangy, without a care.

Sweet Squeeze

In the kitchen, zest goes flying,
A citrus fight, oh, laughing, crying.
Too much juice, the floor is sticky,
In my hair, that's just too tricky.

The neighbors peek to see the ruckus,
A yellow splash, oh what a fuss!
I slip and slide, it's quite absurd,
"Who knew you'd dance with a citrus bird?"

A squeeze, a squirt, a zany game,
Who knew cooking could bring such fame?
With every drop, I jest and tease,
My kitchen antics, the ultimate breeze!

Now my drink's a frothy delight,
With too much tang, it's quite a sight!
So here's to fun in citrus lands,
Where laughter flows and joy expands!

A Slice of Brightness

A sunny slice upon my plate,
Its cheerful hue, I celebrate.
I try to eat, but oh, it squirts,
I laugh so hard, my stomach hurts!

The juice flies high, a flying kiss,
My shirt now holds a citrus mist.
I call my friends, they can't believe,
The games we play, they won't perceive!

A citrus crown atop my head,
I dance around, my friends all fed.
With every giggle, joy will blend,
A fruity feast, there's no end!

My table's set, a cheerful show,
With lemon cakes and drinks that glow.
So here we toast to silly cheer,
With slices bright, we dance and cheer!

Juicy Revelations

In my hand, the fruit does squish,
A funky taste, oh, what a wish!
With every bite, I laugh in glee,
My tart surprise brings jubilee!

I tried to bake a lemon pie,
But ended up with fruit that flies.
My kitchen's now a zany scene,
With citrus everywhere, it's obscene!

My pets join in, they leap and play,
Chasing zest that rolls away.
A game of catch, a yellow chase,
I never knew such citrus grace!

But as I sip this tangy drink,
I smile wide, I cannot blink.
These juicy times, I wouldn't trade,
For all the world, joyous cascade!

Yellow Glow

A golden hue, it shines and glows,
This vibrant fruit, everyone knows.
In silly games, I twirl and spin,
With every laugh, I just can't win!

I roll a lemon down the street,
It takes a turn, it's quite a feat!
Neighbors watch this fruit parade,
Their giggles blend, a fun charade!

I squeeze a bit, oh what a splash,
My friends all laugh, they cannot dash!
"Let's make a drink, oh what a mix!"
With ice and zest, we stir the fix!

So here's my toast to yellow cheer,
With every drop, bring laughter near.
In moments bright, we find our jest,
Life's juicy fun, we are so blessed!

Citrus Whispers

In a garden bright and sunny,
A fruit so bold, it's really funny.
With skins so yellow, like a sun,
It teases us until we run.

A sip of juice, it makes us grin,
The tangy taste, a joyful spin.
We laugh and giggle, can't resist,
This zesty friend, a citrus twist.

From lemonade to cake so sweet,
This playful fruit can't be beat.
With every drop, a burst of cheer,
It brightens days, brings laughter near.

So here's to fun in every bite,
This cheeky fruit, a pure delight.
In every zest, a joke concealed,
A citrus grin, oh how it's healed!

Zestful Revelations

A citrus twist in every tale,
With giggles shared, we'll never fail.
Its tangy prance, a lively scene,
We'll dance around this golden sheen.

Juicy secrets in the sun,
Each slice reveals, oh what fun!
Bright and bold, it steals the show,
In every laugh, the flavors flow.

From morning teas to evening feasts,
This zest brings joy, it never ceases.
It sparkles bright, it twirls with grace,
A sassy fruit, it sets the pace.

So let us squeeze, let out a cheer,
For this zesty muse that draws us near.
In every sip, a pop of joy,
With laughter shared, no room for coy!

Sunshine in a Squeeze

Oh, burst of joy, in every squeeze,
With delightful flavors that tease.
A twist of fate, so tangy and bright,
This yellow sphere is pure delight.

From kitchen to the backyard grill,
It adds a zing that brings a thrill.
With every drop, we laugh and play,
This sunny gem lights up our day.

Citrusy giggles fill the air,
With every drizzle, joy to share.
A frothy drink, a sweetened treat,
In every glass, we dance on our feet.

So here's to fun in every pour,
With zestful hearts, we crave for more.
A squeeze of joy, a splash of cheer,
Let's keep this sunshine ever near!

Radiant Pith

In a world where laughter reigns,
A curious fruit with funny gains.
Its bright attire, an eye-catching sight,
Unleashing giggles, pure delight.

Each little drop, a zesty trick,
With flavors twirling, bold and quick.
We sip and share, a citrus spree,
In silly puns, we all agree.

From scrumptious pies to frothy shakes,
This radiant charm never breaks.
Its laughter bubbles, it loves to tease,
Our hearts alight with citrus ease.

So let's raise a glass, and toast the night,
With every sip, our spirits bright.
In joyful moments, may we bask,
For a playful fruit, is all we ask!

Radiance Unleashed

In a bowl, they sit and grin,
Winking under the kitchen's din.
Zesty jokes they yell and shout,
With a twist, they dance about.

Lemonade plans spin in their head,
Silly thoughts that leap from bed.
A slice of laughter, bright and bold,
Sour stories waiting to be told.

With every squeeze, a giggle comes,
Citrus mischief, drumming drums.
Bright and tangy, they're the jest,
Sour faces surely are the best!

From the fridge, a light they bring,
Daring us to laugh and sing.
With zest and charm, they steal the show,
These cheeky fruits that steal the glow.

Sour Serenity

Resting softly on the shelf,
Cackling softly to themselves.
With a tartness that can't be beat,
They bubble up, not miss a beat!

Citrus giggles fill the air,
In their glow, there's no despair.
Jokes on lips and smiles so bright,
Turning sour into delight.

Slice them up, watch them gleam,
In every punchline lies a dream.
Their yellow zest, a soft embrace,
Happiness in every space.

So here we gather, all around,
With funny tales in tangy sound.
Laughter pours like summer rain,
In this quirky, citrus lane.

Energetic Citrus

Bounding in with zest and glee,
These tiny fruits yell, "Come see!"
Rolls of laughter, quick and spry,
With every twist, they reach the sky.

Jumpy antics, here they come,
Sour antics, oh so fun!
In the blender, dance and spin,
Frothy chaos mixed within.

Lemon cheerleaders, bright and loud,
Tossing seeds among the crowd.
Their jokes are tangy, sharp, and sweet,
A zest-filled party can't be beat!

They challenge limes to a duel,
Flipping jokes, acting the fool.
In this citrus circus, we adopt,
The feeling of joy that can't be stopped.

Illumination in Yellow

Glowing bright upon the table,
Telling tales, oh can't you label?
In their peel, a spark of cheer,
Eager giggles, drawing near.

Shining bright with sunny rays,
They turn dull into a craze.
Every slice reveals a grin,
A party where the fun begins!

Witty puns rolled in the rind,
Cheeky fun that's well-defined.
Sipping juice, we toast to fate,
In joyful moments, we create.

So gather 'round this fruity crew,
Laughing deep, as laughter grew.
Together they shine, vibrant and bold,
In every twist, warm tales unfold.

Citrus Sparks of Joy

In a bowl of yellow cheer,
A citrus grin spreads wide,
Squeezed out giggles fill the air,
As friends and laughter collide.

With every twist and turn,
Juice flies like confetti,
Sour faces turn to smiles,
As we get all sweaty.

Mismatched sips of lemonade,
A funny taste surprise,
Puckered lips and silly pouts,
While everyone just laughs and cries.

As zestful dreams take flight,
Bouncing like a ball,
Citrus joy, an endless joke,
We'll catch it with a call.

Luminous Citrus Journeys.

Under sunny skies we roam,
With citrus peels in hand,
Each twist and turn is filled with laughs,
As we squeeze a bit unplanned.

In a lemonade parade,
Join the fizzy flow,
Sipping joy from silly cups,
As laughter starts to grow.

With tangy tales that spark delight,
And tongues that pucker tight,
We roll down hills of zesty fun,
Chasing the fading light.

As bubbles rise and spirits soar,
Each sip, a wild ride,
Join the journey, hop along,
Where laughter's our guide.

Zestful Whispers

Whispers of zest in the air,
A citrus giggle floats about,
With every sip we share a grin,
And laughter rounds the scout.

Underneath the lemon tree,
Silly tales take flight,
In a citrus comedy show,
The stars come out at night.

Juice drips down chins and shirts,
A zesty artwork spree,
With every squeeze, another laugh,
As fun pours wild and free.

Gather round for zingy chats,
In a cheerful citrus crowd,
Each zesty word a spark of joy,
Within our laughter loud.

Citrus Firefly

In the twilight of citrus dreams,
A firefly flits and spins,
With bubbly grace it twinkles bright,
Sharing where the fun begins.

Sipping sweetened sparkly drinks,
We chase the night away,
Each laugh ignites a zesty flare,
In our funny cabaret.

With giggles whirling like confetti,
And puns that sweetly sting,
The world is bright with citrus hues,
As we dance and sing.

So follow that firefly glow,
As the laughter starts to fly,
Embrace the humor in each sip,
Beneath the starry sky.

Hope in Every Slice

In the kitchen, chaos reigns,
A citrus ball that never wanes.
Slicing through with joy and glee,
Zesty dreams are all we see.

Rolling on the countertop,
A tiny dance, it just won't stop.
With a twist and a little squirt,
Laughter rises, no room for hurt.

When life hands us a tart surprise,
We juggle fruit, not compromise.
A splash of yellow, a wink of fate,
We turn the frown to something great.

So grab your knife, don't be shy,
With each cut, let giggles fly.
A lemon's tale, sweet and bright,
In every slice, there's pure delight.

Joyful Zest

A citrus party on the plate,
Where joy and flavor never wait.
With pips that dance and rinds that shine,
We toast to fun, it's lemon time!

Lemonade flows, a fizzy cheer,
Bubbling laughter fills the sphere.
When life gets sour, don't you fret,
Add some sparkle, never forget.

A zesty wink, a playful tease,
Lemon meringue brings all the breeze.
With every bite, a burst of fun,
Who knew this fruit could make us run?

So let's all squeeze out joy today,
I'll share my zest, come out and play.
With laughter fresh as morning dew,
Let's make some memories, just us two.

The Sun's Sharp Embrace

In gardens where the laughter grows,
Sunlight kisses petals, glows.
Citrus leaves wave in the breeze,
Giving life to all, with ease.

A sunny day, a fruity scheme,
We toss and catch, a citrus dream.
With every drop, we twirl and sway,
Making lemonade from the day.

Bright and bold, a sight so keen,
Nature's joke, it's quite the scene.
With flavors bursting, smiles are made,
In sunlit laughter, worries fade.

Let joy be squeezed from every slice,
A burst of cheer, oh, so nice!
With friends around and zest in hand,
We dance through life, just as we planned.

Vivid Citrine Melodies

In a bowl, a medley sings,
Citrus notes on vibrant wings.
With every splash, the giggles soar,
Lemon tunes, we can't ignore.

Twist and turn, the zest will play,
Creating laughter through the day.
A tart surprise, then sweet retreat,
The music swells with every beat.

From kitchen maestros to silly chefs,
We play with flavors, no need for preps.
With every slice, a tale unfolds,
Joy in citrus, life it holds.

So raise a glass, let's celebrate,
In vivid colors, it's never late.
With melodies as bright as sun,
In every drop, our laughter's spun.

Ripening Radiance

In the garden, green and bold,
A fruit so bright, a sight to behold,
With zest that tickles, a laugh for sure,
Makes sour faces feel less demure.

A twist of fate on a sunny day,
With puns galore, come out to play,
A citrus giggle, a jovial cheer,
Bringing sunshine, far and near.

Juicy jests in every bite,
Sour and sweet, pure delight,
A laughter burst, oh what fun,
Bellyaches when the day is done.

Bright skins with secrets to unwind,
Jokes wrapped up, with flavors combined,
In this fruit, joy's fresh allure,
Makes ordinary moments feel less obscure.

Sunkissed Delight

In orchards bright, the laughter spills,
With every slice, a tickling thrill,
Sunkissed wonders, oh what a treat,
Makes even dull days feel quite sweet.

A quirky splash, in lemonade cheer,
Giggles dance as summer draws near,
Puns take flight with every zest,
In this game of fruit, we're all guests.

A yellow glow, from shrub to glass,
Witty quips, as moments pass,
Seeded songs, in a picnic spread,
With silly faces, laughter is fed.

Bright joy blooms, in the sweetest bite,
Craving humor, morning to night,
As we sip on this cheery cheer,
Sunkissed flavors keep smiles near.

Vibrant Spectrum

A splash of yellow, a dash of fun,
With every squeeze, the giggles run,
Citrus dreams in a punchy cheer,
Bringing grins from ear to ear.

Sour jokes with a fruity twist,
Every drop, too fun to resist,
In bowls of joy, we mix and blend,
The laugh parade starts, no need to pretend.

Fragrant shenanigans, bright and bold,
Zesty stories of legends told,
Between the laughs and golden glows,
Laughter seeps where sweetness flows.

Vibrant moments, a simple spark,
Squeezed and shared in the park,
A citrus burst, a mood set right,
In laughter's glow, all feels so bright.

Brightness Within

Beneath the skin, a treasure hides,
In quips and giggles, fun abides,
When life gives you fruit, take a bite,
And watch the world burst into light.

A twist and shout, the zest reveals,
The humor packed, how it appeals,
With every drop, a happy cheer,
Brightness flows, the soul draws near.

Juicy tales from citrus skies,
With laughter loud, as daylight flies,
The tangy treats make spirits lift,
A cheerful heart, the perfect gift.

So crack a smile, and share the glee,
In citrus fun, we're wild and free,
With every slice, let joy begin,
For in this fruit, there's brightness within.

Citrine Vibes

In a land where citrus dreams dance bright,
Lemons twirl in the sun, what a sight!
They giggle and wiggle, with zest they run,
Squeezing joy from the rays, oh what fun!

With a splash of yellow, smiles appear,
Lemonade rivers flowing near.
Friendships bubbling like fizzy bees,
Tickling our senses, hearts at ease.

Peeling back laughter, a twist of a rind,
Sour notes weaving, oh so entwined.
A citrus parade, with hats made of zest,
Who knew such fruit could be nature's jest!

Under the sun's warmth, it's clear to see,
A world infused with lemon's decree.
From tart to sweet, we all must agree,
Citrine vibes bursting, wild and free!

Tangy Solstice

On the day of the sun's grand debut,
Lemons sing songs in brilliant hue.
Dancing on branches, with glee they sway,
Spreading their giggles, brightening the day.

A sorcery brewed in a jug so round,
Sip after sip, joy and laughs abound.
Pies cooling on windows, a citrusy tease,
For every sneeze, a lemon's bright squeeze!

Spinning like tops in a tangy delight,
Friends gather 'round for the zesty bite.
Games made of laughter and lemony cheer,
The world turns bright, when they're near!

In this solstice of sun and silliness found,
We'll mix our smiles on the merry-go-round.
So raise your cup, let the citrus flow,
Tangy adventures are sure to grow!

Piquant Journeys

Once upon a time, a lemon took flight,
Over hills and valleys, day turned to night.
With friends from the orchard, they flew in a row,
Chasing the sunset, putting on a show.

They sailed through the clouds, all zesty and bold,
Sharing their secrets, stories untold.
One slipped on a cloud, what a comical sight!
Landing in laughter, with citrus delight!

Ode to the zest, the journeys we make,
With peels of joy, for our laughter's sake.
Each twist in the road, a new lemony sage,
In the book of our lives, we scribble the page!

So gather your friends, let the fun never cease,
In these piquant journeys, may joy find peace.
Adventure awaits with a glint in your eye,
Let the lemony laughter reach up to the sky!

Lively Essence

In the market of dreams, where lemons abound,
Bright faces gather, such fun can be found.
With zest in their hearts and giggles so wide,
Lively essence blooms, let's take a ride!

Sipping the sunshine, oh what a splash!
Lemon sorbet dancing, in a colorful dash.
With each tangy scoop, we burst into grin,
A riot of flavors, let the games begin!

Wobbling in laughter, a lemony tune,
Underneath the stars, by the silvered moon.
From trees to our tummies, the flavor sets free,
Squeezing delight from each moment in glee!

So here's to the citrus, a lively embrace,
In the essence of joy, we find our place.
With friends by our side, and laughter so bright,
Together we'll dance, through the long summer night!

Sun-Soaked Moments

Under the sun, we laugh and play,
Sipping something tangy all day.
A splash of laughter, a twist of lime,
Dancing to the rhythm, oh, what a time!

Bright yellow skies, our joy ignites,
Juggling citrus, oh what sights!
With every squirt, our giggles grow,
A zesty tale, in the sun's warm glow!

Flip-flops flapping, our feast in reach,
Sunkissed skin, a zesty peach.
In this moment, pure delight,
We giggle till it's time for night!

So grab a glass, fill it up high,
Watch the bubbles dance and fly.
Sun-soaked memories, let's embrace,
In this citrus-fueled, joyful space!

Sparkling Zest

Fizzing bubbles, a joyous spree,
A dash of mischief, just you and me.
Carefree laughter, a playful jest,
A splash of color, we're feeling blessed!

Squeeze out the smiles, let the fun unfurl,
With every pop, let laughter twirl.
The sweetness lingers, oh what a twist,
In this zesty, bubbly, sunshine mist!

So here we are, dancing in glee,
With juicy jokes, like honey from a bee.
Each sip a giggle, a delightful tease,
Living our best, with such fizzy ease!

As twilight falls, our spirits clear,
Chasing bubbles, and spreading cheer.
In sparkling zest, we find a light,
The silly moments that feel so right!

Luminous Sunshine

Waking to warmth, the sun's embrace,
Chasing shadows, a merry race.
With grins so wide, we take a chance,
In a zesty world, let's jiggle and dance!

Golden beams, and giddying thrills,
Citrus scent on the windowsills.
Brighten the day with a zany song,
Laughter is where we all belong!

As rays peek through, we play and spin,
Each joyful moment keeps drawing us in.
Between the giggles and silly pranks,
We raise our cups and toast with thanks!

Morning to dusk, let's keep it bright,
With hearts aglow, we'll take flight.
In this luminous swirl of joy,
Every twinkling smile, oh what a ploy!

A Drop of Joy

Just a squeeze, and the world's aglow,
A splash of laughter, a little show.
Witty banter with zestful flair,
Each chuckle shared, floating in air!

In silly hats, we twirl around,
In our citrus kingdom, joy is found.
With every drop and mischief's tease,
We cultivate giggles with wonderful ease!

Bright flavors mix, a dance divine,
Tickling senses, oh how we shine!
With playful pouts and citrus-y cheer,
Each blink and wink, we bring the cheer!

So raise a toast to the little things,
For every drop, a new joy brings.
In this zesty life where we both play,
Let's laugh and twirl, come what may!

Lemonade Dreams

In a glass, a chatter bold,
Fizz and pop, tales unfold,
Twisting straws and sips that gleam,
Oh, the joy in lemonade dreams!

A lemon slice with cheeky grin,
Winks at you, come on, jump in!
Sweet or sour, who can decide?
Bubbles dance, let laughter glide.

Sunshine syrup, giggles afloat,
Floating ice cubes like a boat,
Absurd ways to sip so bright,
Gulps of glee, pure delight!

In this cup, a carnival waits,
Twirling flavors, funny fates,
When life gives fruits, let's not wait,
Join the fun—just celebrate!

Scented Sunshine

Zesty whispers fill the air,
Golden glow with citrus flair,
Juicy scent of mirthful spree,
Lemon zest is wild and free!

Dancing peels on kitchen floors,
Zingy pranks behind closed doors,
Giggles bubble like a brew,
Scented sunshine, pure and true.

Juggling fruits, a sight to see,
A squirt of glee from playfulness spree,
Twisted faces, sour surprise,
Brightening moods, oh how time flies!

In every pout, a chuckle waits,
Frothy floats with silly states,
Living life, a fruity cheer,
With scented sunshine, laugh sincere!

Brilliant Squeeze

A citrus twist, so bold and bright,
A brilliant squeeze, pure delight,
Lemon chuckles, tangy tease,
In every drop, the joy will please!

Funny faces when you sip,
A soured wink, a playful quip,
Jars of zest, laughter ignites,
Bottled giggles, magical sights.

Whisked together in sheer glee,
Sour notes and wild jubilee,
Citrus capers, snappy fun,
Brilliant antics, one by one.

Under the sun, with zest we play,
Life's a laugh in this grand ballet,
Sip by sip, we seize the day,
In every squeeze, joy's here to stay!

Echo of Citrus

Bouncing echoes, bright and spry,
Sour giggles flutter by,
Citrus laughter fills the space,
In every sip, a silly chase!

Tangy whispers, playful tease,
Jokes spilled out on summer breeze,
Lemons roll with laughter loud,
Echoes dance, we're citrus proud!

Squeezing joy with every drop,
Funny faces that never stop,
Bright yellow rays, a jester's cheer,
Every gulp brings friends near!

Let's splash around, a zesty crew,
With echoes of fun, we'll renew,
Life's a game, so drink it quick,
In lemon laughter, time's a trick!

Vivid Infusion

In a bowl of zesty cheer,
Slices dance without a fear,
Laughter bubbles, bright and bold,
A splash of joy, a taste of gold.

Zingy juice drips everywhere,
Sticky hands and happy air,
With every twist, a giggle bursts,
Quenching thirsts and quenching firsts.

A twist of fate, a citrus prank,
Who knew this could fill the tank?
Sours to sweet, like magic spells,
Tales of fruit that laughter tells.

Peel the joy, unwrap the fun,
Fun's not done, the game's begun!
In this zestful, fruity play,
Every moment's a cabaret.

Citrus Sunburst

A citrus caper starts today,
With zest that tickles all the way,
Sunshine drips from every slice,
A laugh erupts, oh how nice!

In a glass that spins and swirls,
Joyful giggles, dizzy twirls,
Sipping smiles with every sip,
Life's a zestful, fruity trip.

With peels that fly like confetti,
Banter sweet, and laughter steady,
Fruit salad jokes in every bite,
Citrus giggles, pure delight.

A splash of green, a dash of fun,
Citrus rays, we're on the run!
In this garden of chortling glee,
Lemon laughter sets us free.

Vibrant Whirl

Round and round the citrus spin,
Bubbly giggles, making grins,
A whirl of zest, a wild ride,
Fragrant joy we cannot hide.

Skip and hop with lemon zest,
In this game, we're all the best,
Slice the laughter, serve it up,
A vibrant zing in every cup.

With every chuckle, bright and loud,
Citrus fun, we're so proud,
Not a sour face around,
Just bright smiles and laughter found.

Nature's candy, sweet and bright,
Life's a dance in pure delight,
Join the party, come and see,
In this fruit-filled jubilee.

Bright Bounty

Golden globe of sour sweet,
A tasty tale beneath our feet,
Roll the fruit, watch laughter bloom,
Filling up the vibrant room.

Chasing juice from sunlit rays,
Silly faces in a daze,
Sipping joy, no time for frowns,
Citrus capers, giggling clowns.

Squeeze the day for all it's worth,
Wrap our hearts in sunny mirth,
With every burst, we take a swig,
Bouncing high, oh so big!

A bright bounty of laughter here,
With every squirt, we shift the gear,
Join the fun, don't miss this lark,
In the joy of citrus spark.

Radiant Rind

In a zesty land of yellow glow,
Silly citrus plays a show.
Juggling pies with a twist of zest,
Laughter rises, it's the best!

Brighty fruit in a comical dance,
Making faces, they take a chance.
With lemon hats and giggles loud,
A citrus circus, oh so proud!

In the garden, a sticky plight,
A bee got lost in the tangy sight.
With a buzz, he tried to sing,
But all he got was a sour fling!

So here's to rind, so vivid and keen,
In jester's garb, it takes the scene.
With laughter sweet, we'll share a grin,
For citrus fun, let's all jump in!

A Burst of Sun

Out in the grove, a comical beam,
Sunshine lemon with a gleamy dream.
He wears a smile, big and wide,
With juice that bursts, full of pride!

Frolicking in the morning light,
Sipping tangy, feeling just right.
Tickling taste buds with a zing,
In this orchard, it's a swing!

A squirrel passed, a thief in flight,
Took a lemon, oh what a sight!
He slipped and fell with a citrus grin,
His fuzzy tail all covered in skin!

Join the laugh, embrace the fun,
For every day is a burst of sun.
With silliness ripe and joy that flows,
In yellow fields, the happiness grows!

Golden Essence

Golden slices, a funny affair,
Pies and tarts float in the air.
Dancing chefs with flour on nose,
Creating wonders, as humor grows!

A jester lemon, he juggles right,
With giggles bursting, quite the sight.
Chasing bubbles with zestful cheer,
A citrus laugh, loud and clear!

Peeled and punned, they tell a tale,
When life gives fruit, you should set sail.
With every twirl, a story's spun,
In a whirl of laughs, we have our fun!

So let us squeeze out every drop,
With every giggle, we'll never stop.
In golden hues, joy will dance,
With every laugh, we twirl and prance!

Tangy Illuminations

Under the moon, a citrus play,
Lemons glow in the night, hooray!
With melodious laughs, they shine so bright,
Turning even shadows into light.

A clumsy clown, on a lemon so round,
Trips and tumbles, his antics abound.
Bouncing off walls with a streak of zest,
In a cackle, we fondly jest!

Awkward fruit in hats divine,
They tell us tales over a glass of brine.
With sassy puns and a tangy tone,
In this citrus realm, we're never alone!

So raise a glass, toast to the night,
For the tangy fun is a pure delight.
With lemons bright, let laughter flow,
In every sip, let the good vibes grow!

Brightness in a Peel

In a garden bright, I found a treat,
A zesty orb beneath my feet.
With a wink and giggle, it rolled away,
Chasing it seemed like a game to play.

With a splash of juice, it danced in delight,
Turning my frown into sheer light.
A citrus caper, a vibrant scene,
Never thought fruit could be this keen!

When life hands you yellow, make it your goal,
To squeeze out some joy and brighten your soul.
For even a peel can inspire a grin,
Who knew such mischief could lurk within?

So here's to the fruit with a tangy twist,
A laugh for each slice, you get the gist.
It's a citrus smile, oh what a steal,
The secrets contained in a simple peel.

Tangy Awakening

In the morning sun, a bright little sphere,
Called to me softly, 'Come, have no fear!'
I squeezed and I squirted, what a wild ride,
Turns out this fruit had a zestful side!

It juggled my worries with each little squish,
Turning my frown into a funny wish.
With each sour laugh, my troubles did fade,
Who knew a simple fruit could upstage?

So next time you feel like life's getting dull,
Just grab a bright fruit, give it a pull.
Embrace the tang, let your spirits rise,
For laughter's the best, in citrus disguise.

And when you're done, share a giggle or two,
For joy multiplies when it's given its due.
Each drop's an adventure, remember this spree,
And wink at your fruit with gleeful glee!

Golden Drops of Joy

A golden orb sat upon the shelf,
I thought to myself, 'Let's sample this elf!'
With a twist and a turn, it popped with a grin,
Who knew such a ball could cause this din?

Dripping sunshine, it sashayed about,
Creating sweet chaos, that's what it's about!
Each drop a burst of glittering fun,
In the silly dance of a citrus-y run.

As I took a sip, oh what a surprise,
Joy exploded, like fireworks in the skies.
It giggled and wiggled as I gave it a squeeze,
Who knew such laughter could come from the squeeze?

So celebrate with zest, my friends, take a chance,
Let the golden drops lead you to dance.
For in every juicy flick of a skin,
There's a party of laughter waiting within!

Essence of Citrus Dreams

In the dream of a fruit, so bright and bold,
Lived a juicy creature with stories untold.
It tumbled through gardens, making a scene,
Sipping on sunshine, feeling like a queen.

With each little drop, a giggle would swell,
As the fruit spun tales they could hardly tell.
Tickling taste buds with magic so sweet,
Turning dull moments into a treat.

When life starts to sour, and things feel unclear,
Just grab this orb friend; make laughter your spear.
Its essence brings smiles like confetti in air,
Creating a rhythm that's tender and rare.

So venture forth boldly, let zesty winds blow,
And dance in the dreams of the citrusy glow.
For laughter and fruit are a pair divine,
In this wacky circus, let your joy shine!

Juiced Inspiration

In the fridge, so bright and bold,
A zesty fruit, a tale untold.
I squeezed my thoughts, oh what a mess,
Out poured ideas, I must confess.

A splash of tang, a dash of fun,
My brain awoke, oh how it spun!
I stirred the pot, with seeds of cheer,
Who knew such joy could happen here?

With every twist, I made a rhyme,
The pulpy beats, they danced in time.
So if you're stuck, don't you despair,
Just grab a fruit and shake the air!

Now lemons laugh, they roll and play,
In my wild dreams, they shout, 'Hooray!'
Ideas sprout with every squeeze,
Juiced inspiration, oh, what a tease!

Chasing Brightness

A yellow orb that lights my day,
In fields of green, I prance and sway.
With every grin, I chase the sun,
A fruity mission; oh, what fun!

I tripped on clouds of citrus glee,
With sticky fingers, I felt so free.
The laughter bubbled, bright and loud,
In this sweet pursuit, I felt so proud.

I danced with sparks of zesty cheer,
Creating joy, I had no fear.
With every zing, my spirit soared,
Chasing brightness, I was adored!

So join the romp, don't stand aside,
In this lemon land, we take a ride.
With goofy grins, we leap and hop,
Chasing brightness, we'll never stop!

Lemonade Daydreams

In a pitcher bright, with ice aglow,
I mixed my thoughts, oh what a show!
With sugar swirls and citrus crush,
Daydreams froth in a fizzy rush.

I sipped the sun, I spun around,
In lemonade land, pure joy is found.
With straw in hand, I made a wish,
For silly dreams in each sweet swish.

I saw the clouds in shades of gold,
Waving at me, their stories bold.
The world was bright, a punchy scene,
In lemonade daydreams, life's a dream!

So quench your thirst, dive into cheer,
With every sip, bring magic near.
Let's toast to fun, to laughs and beams,
In this cool world of daydreams!

Golden Kisses

Underneath the sunny skies,
Golden fruits catch happy eyes.
With every bite, a burst of cheer,
Sweet and tangy, come gather near.

A playful dance of zest and grin,
In sticky hugs, let the fun begin.
The juiciness wraps around like bliss,
A journey starts with a citrus kiss.

Bouncing lemons on the ground,
Giggling sprites all around.
In golden hues, we paint our days,
With laughter bright in lemony ways!

So come and laugh, don't be shy,
With golden kisses, reach for the sky.
In this fruity world, let's play and twirl,
Where joy is tossed and life's a whirl!

A Glimmer of Tartness

In the fridge, a yellow guest,
With a grin, it likes to jest.
Pucker up, it starts to laugh,
A dance that's pure, no need for math.

Zesty notes in every sip,
A citrus twist that likes to slip.
Its humor's sharp, but oh so sweet,
A fizzy tale, a charming treat.

When life gives you a citrus gift,
Just take a sip, let worries lift.
In tangy prance, we find our cheer,
A wobbly wobble, loud and clear.

With every slice, we giggle out,
A squeeze of joy, without a doubt.
Pies and drinks, they call with glee,
A citrus crown for you and me.

Squeeze of Serenity

A splash of sunshine, bright and bold,
In every drop, a story told.
Witty zings in each small bite,
A sour laugh dances with delight.

Bubble up in joyous cheer,
As flavors twist and disappear.
A citrus chuckle fills the air,
Embrace the tart, throw away despair.

When life's a mess, just catch a spark,
In tartness, you'll find a little lark.
Squeeze it tighter, let it be,
Nature's prank, a taste of free!

With every zest, you'll see it glow,
A potion brewed, a show to show.
Dance with fruit, the laugh parade,
In every sip, joy's masquerade.

Flavorful Revelations

A burst of flavor, oh so bright,
Turns frowns around, from day to night.
Zesty whispers, a citrus tease,
With every drop, we pair with cheese.

Tickle your taste, let senses soar,
In fruity puns, we find much more.
A splash of wit in muddled glass,
Laugh with each sip, let moments pass.

Spinning tales of sprightly zest,
Made for laughter, life's greatest jest.
With every twist, a spark ignites,
Reviving hearts on lonely nights.

Pull out the juicer, let it squeeze,
You'll find the joy in every ease.
Mix it up, and let it flow,
In every taste, a chance to glow.

Sparkling Drops of Delight

Glimmering bubbles in a glass,
A funny story, a sassy sass.
With every fizz, a laugh we get,
A tickling sip we won't forget.

Citrus dance, it swirls and spins,
In perfect sync, the laughter wins.
It twirls around, a zesty plot,
A sip and giggle, hit the spot!

With every sip, we find the fun,
Our taste buds jump, the race begun.
So pop that cork and let it flow,
A joyful chant we now bestow.

Squeeze that grin, unleash your mind,
In tangy bliss, true joy we find.
With sparkling drops, let laughter bloom,
In every room, it clears the gloom.

Vibrant Harvest of Life

In a garden bright where fruits abound,
Zesty wonders grow from the ground.
A slip on zest, oh what a sight,
Laughing as I take a bite!

Bouncing lemons, round and bold,
Tales of laughter, sweetly told.
Sour faces, smiles around,
In this harvest, joy is found!

Pies and drinks, a tangy spree,
Who knew fruit could be so free?
Peeling back a citrus grin,
Let the funny fest begin!

Oddball lemons rolled in glee,
In mischief's grip, come dance with me!
Chasing shadows, bright and spry,
In this orchard, laughter flies!

Juicy Moments

On a picnic, what a blast,
With juicy tales that hold you fast.
Splat! The juice flew everywhere,
Sticky fun, oh, do we care?

Neighbors gasp at our wild thrift,
As we juggle citrus with a lift.
Juicy moments, we'll recall,
When laughter rises, we stand tall.

Citrus hats and slippery shoes,
Impromptu games, not one to lose!
Sipping drinks that are all mixed,
Life's a play, and we're all fixed!

Bring on the zest, the sweet delight,
In every moment, day or night.
What's the fuss? Just join the fun,
Grapefruits and jokes, we've just begun!

A Tangy Dance

In the kitchen, everyone pranced,
Chopping up the fruits, we danced.
A citrus twist, a wobbly jig,
Blend and mix, oh how we dig!

Lemonade rivers flow with glee,
Wobbling tables, can you see?
A tangy beat that makes us smile,
Shake those hips, let's stay a while!

Spill the zest and laugh away,
Citrus peels make for a play.
Fruits collide in colorful flings,
In the whirl, joy surely sings!

Grab a friend and take a chance,
Join this silly lemon dance.
We'll squeeze the day with silly flair,
Tangled in laughter, without a care!

Sun-Kissed Memories

Golden rays on the fruit we made,
Sour dreams in sunshine laid.
Rolling laughter through the air,
Mishaps turning into rare!

Lemonade spills on a sunburned knee,
A sticky tale, just you and me.
Memories sparkle, as our drinks overflow,
Crafting tales that steal the show!

Zesty dishes on the table,
Complete silliness, if we're able!
With every splash, and every bite,
We toast to laughter, pure delight!

Sunset comes, but we're not done,
Chasing shadows, oh what fun!
In every sip, a giggle glows,
In sunny dreams, our friendship grows!

www.ingramcontent.com/pod-product-compliance
Lightning Source LLC
Chambersburg PA
CBHW050307120526
44590CB00016B/2528